Growing Up Where Jesus Lived

Joan Ripley Smith

A Beka Book® Pensacola, FL 32523-9100
an affiliate ministry of PENSACOLA CHRISTIAN COLLEGE®

Growing Up Where Jesus Lived
Second Edition

Staff Credits
Author: Joan Ripley Smith
Illustrators: John Ball, Matthew Sample II, Joan Ripley Smith

A Beka Book, a Christian textbook ministry affiliated with Pensacola Christian College, is designed to meet the need for Christian textbooks and teaching aids. The purpose of this publishing ministry is to help Christian schools reach children and young people for the Lord and train them in the Christian way of life.

Cataloging Data
Smith, Joan Ripley.
Growing up where Jesus lived / written and illustrated by Joan Ripley Smith; John Ball; Matthew Sample II.
100 p.; col. ill.; 23 cm. + teacher's ed. (A Beka Book reading program)
For grade 2.
1. Reading, Elementary. 2. Readers, Elementary.
III. Ball, John. IV. Sample, Matthew, II. V. A Beka Book, Inc.
Library of Congress: PE1119.S65 G76 2006
Dewey System: 428.6

Contents

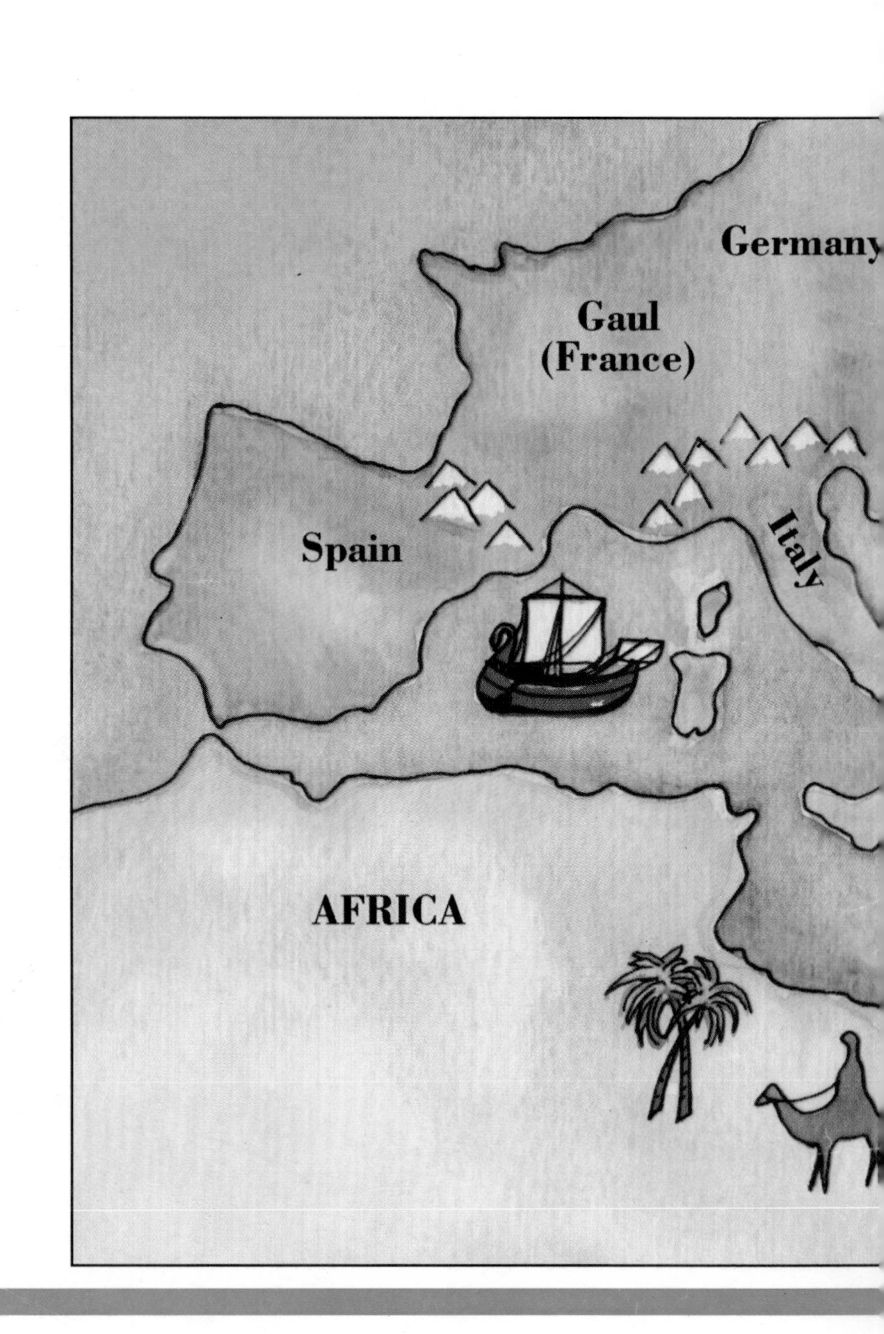
Germany
Gaul
(France)
Spain
Italy
AFRICA

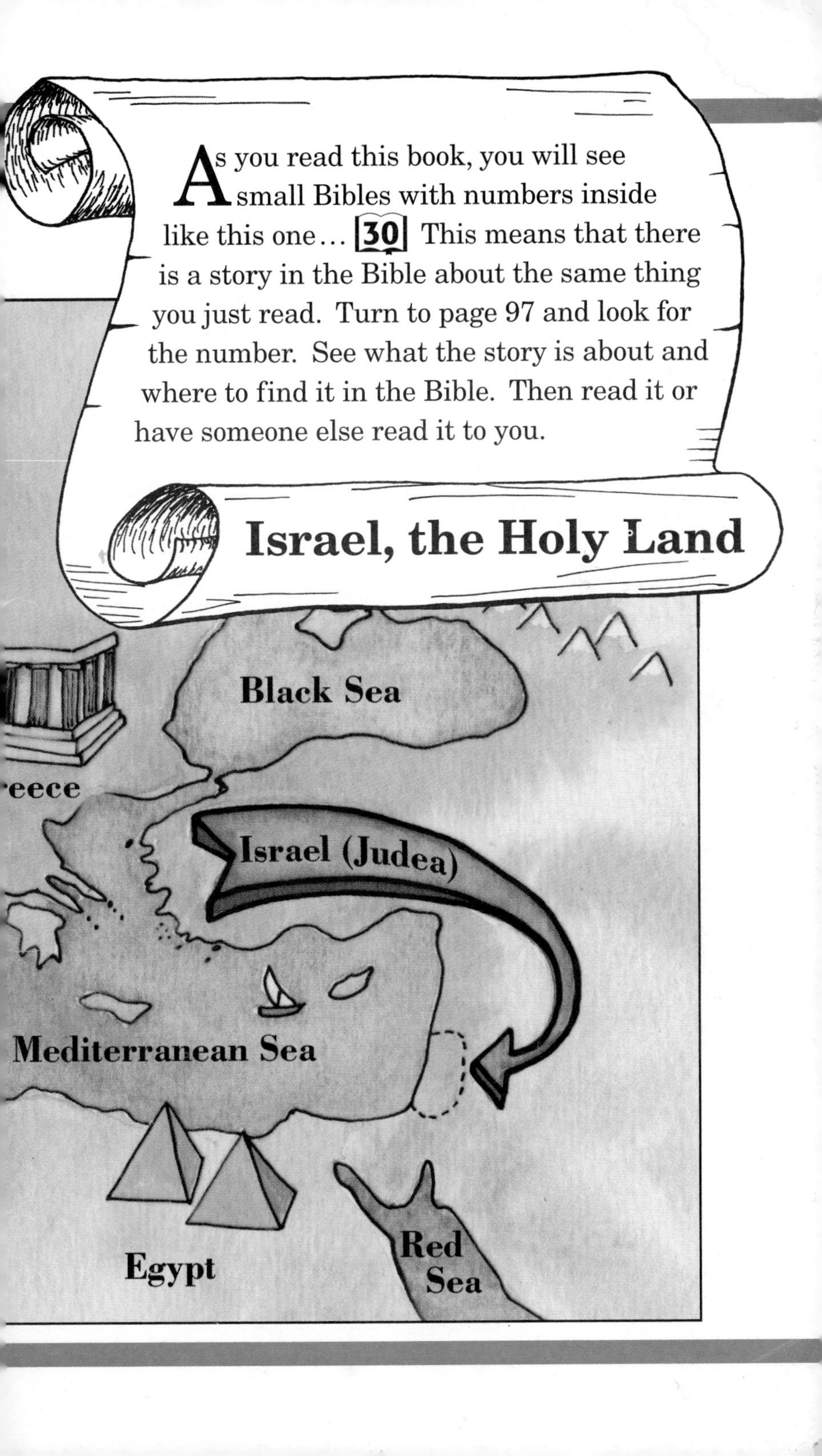
As you read this book, you will see small Bibles with numbers inside like this one... 30 This means that there is a story in the Bible about the same thing you just read. Turn to page 97 and look for the number. See what the story is about and where to find it in the Bible. Then read it or have someone else read it to you.
Israel, the Holy Land
Black Sea
eece
Israel (Judea)
Mediterranean Sea
Egypt
Red
Sea

Introduction

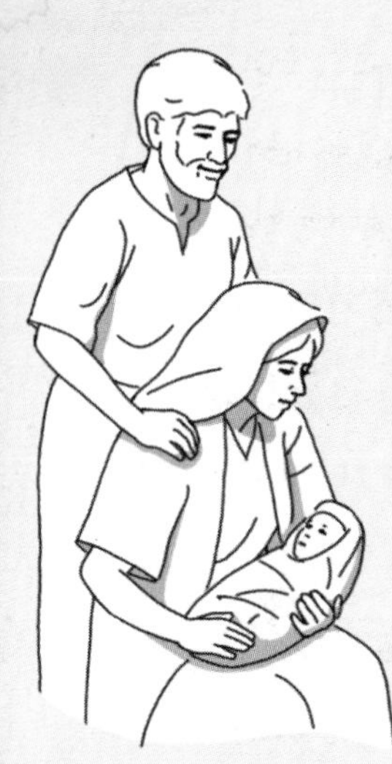

Almost two thousand years ago, God sent his Son, Jesus, to live on the earth. The Bible tells us that He came as a newborn baby to a woman named Mary, who was married to a man named Joseph. Mary and Joseph lived in Israel, or the Holy Land.

Israel was a tiny land at the eastern end of the Mediterranean Sea. *Israel* is the name of the country today. A bird flying high above the land could see it all at one time! Though it was small, the land had all these things: high, snowy mountains and the Dead Sea (the lowest place in the whole world); dry deserts and thick forests; wild jungles and rocky cliffs with caves; the Mediterranean seashore; a huge lake called the Sea of Galilee; and the Jordan River, which ran through the middle of the land.

Many animals lived in the Holy Land. Donkeys, camels, sheep, and goats could be seen everywhere. And when Jesus lived there, there were many wild animals, too.

Lions, bears, wolves, leopards, hyenas, and wild boars could all be found in that land. When Jesus was a boy, Israel was a beautiful and interesting place in which to grow up.

Even though He was the Son of God, Jesus lived in the same kind of house, ate the same kind of food, and wore the same kind of clothes as the children who were His neighbors. In this book you will find out what it was like to grow up in Israel the way Jesus did two thousand years ago.

Chapter 1

Where Would You Live?

In Israel there were only a few big cities. Jerusalem was the largest one. There were many small towns, though, and even more villages. Jesus lived in one of these tiny villages with His parents and His brothers and sisters. The village was called Nazareth. Only a few hundred people lived there when Jesus was a boy. There were many other villages in Israel that were like Nazareth.

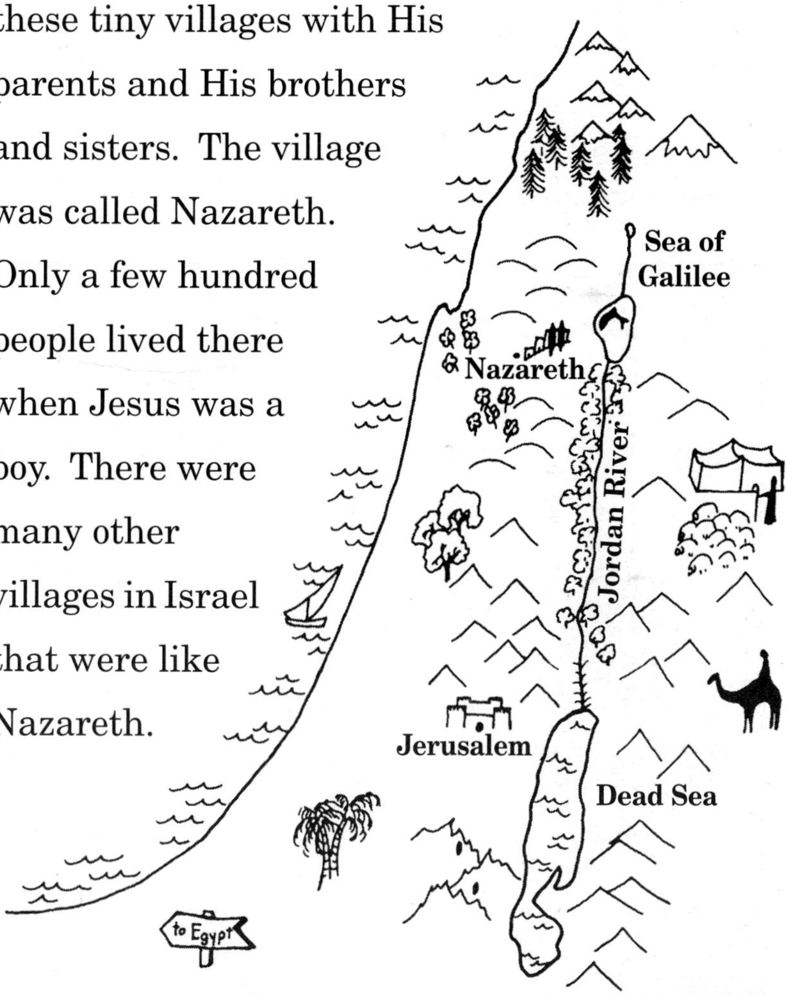

Few rich people lived in these small villages. Many of the men were farmers. The farmers were poor, but their families always had plenty of good food to eat.

The families lived close together so they could all be near the village well and so they could help protect each other from robbers.

Early in the morning, the farmers took their donkeys or oxen to the fields. Sometimes they had to walk a long way. They worked in their fields all day, using the animals to help plow or to carry things. At sunset, the farmers and their animals walked back to the village to be with their families.

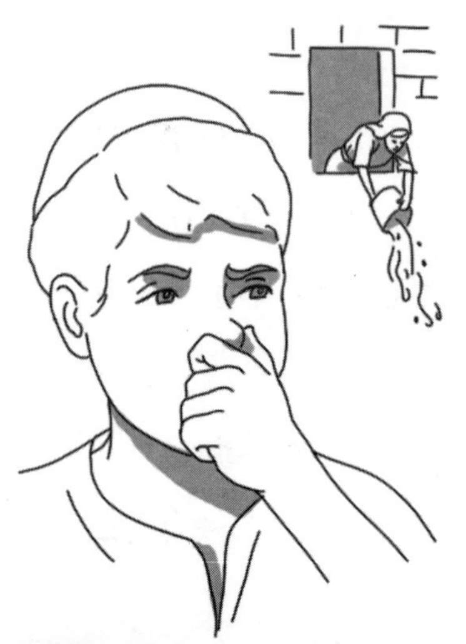

The streets in the villages were not paved. After a rain, they would be a muddy mess. In the summer, they were dusty. People dumped their garbage and dirty water in the street. Because of this, there was often a bad smell.

Most of the streets were very narrow. People sometimes had to step into a doorway as a donkey loaded with bundles passed by.

There were dogs lying in the streets, but they were not pets. These yellow wolflike dogs spent their time sleeping, barking at each other, and eating the garbage in the streets. To call a person a dog was a terrible insult.

The houses on the street were very plain looking. Most people just thought of their house as a safe place to sleep and a place to be protected from the rain and sun. They stayed outside as much as they could.

The windows facing the street were high

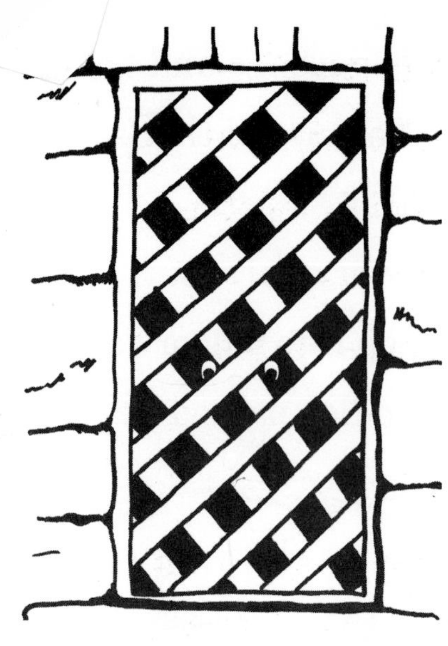

and covered with thin strips of wood called *lattice.* From the street, you could not see inside, but the people inside could see out.

Most houses were made of mud bricks or of stones held together with mud. The rich people had houses made of stones cut into square shapes.

The inside walls of the houses were plastered and covered with white lime to make them clean looking. There were no pictures decorating the walls. It was thought that having a picture might tempt someone to worship what was in the picture instead of worshiping God.

In some poor homes, the floor was just pressed mud. It had to be swept every day and sprinkled with water to keep it from getting too dusty. A better floor would be made of lime and pebbles (a mixture like cement) or of slabs of stone fitted together. It would be easy to lose something small in the cracks of this kind of floor. 1

The front door was made of thick wood. Some doors had a heavy iron ring on the outside for a knocker and a lock that was opened with a large key. The windows had shutters that were closed at night.

If you lived in Israel at this time, you would probably not have had special rooms for the bathroom or kitchen. In fact, many families lived in a house that had only one room. They may have kept some animals in the house with them. Sheep, goats, and maybe even a donkey or a cow would sleep in one end of the room, which was a step lower than the rest of the room. If you lived in a home like this, you would be used to the smell and noise. It would be fun to play with the animals. Your parents might let you make a pet of a baby lamb that lived in your house. Maybe it could even sleep with you.

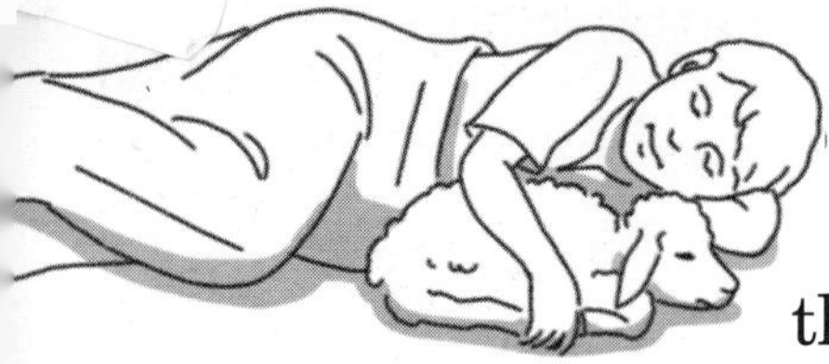

The roof on most houses was made of mud pressed over some branches or reeds. The branches rested on a few large wooden beams. The mud had to be smoothed out and pressed with a stone roller several times a year. This special roller was usually kept on the roof. Sometimes after a heavy rain, the roof would leak. In the middle of the night you might have to get up and move your bed to a dry place. Since the roof was made of mud, sometimes grass would grow on top of your house.

All houses were supposed to have a low

stone wall around the roof so no one would fall off. There were stairs up to the rooftops since people went there often.

Why would you go up to the rooftop?

You could store things up there. You could dry raisins and figs there. You could sleep there on a hot night. You could go on the rooftop to see something that was happening in the street. You could go there to study or pray. Since the rooftops sometimes were joined, you could get to a friend's house that way.

In the summer, some people made a little booth out of leaves and branches for sleeping on the rooftop. Others built a room of stone or brick which could be used for a guest room. A rich family might build several rooms on the roof. They would call this their summer house, and the house below would be their winter house.

A house with more than one room

downstairs would have a courtyard, with the rooms built around it. The courtyard was a place where you could be outdoors but inside the house at the same time. Your courtyard might have a garden of shady trees and flowering bushes.

Sometimes several families shared a

courtyard. Then it would be a busy place. The men would load and unload their donkeys there. The women might do their laundry or cooking in the courtyard.

It would be fun to eat a meal there on a sunny day. On a cold day you could warm your hands over a fire burning in your courtyard. It would be a good place to play. You could even take a bath there!

Some courtyards had a cistern. This was a large rock-lined hole where rainwater was collected. Special drains carried the water from the rooftop to the cistern. You could use that water instead of getting water at the well every day.

If your family were poor, you wouldn't have much furniture in your house. For sleeping and sitting, your would have only mats made of wool or reeds. At night, the mats were spread out on the floor in a row. Your father would sleep at one end, your mother at the other, and you and your brothers and sisters would sleep in between. [2]

Families who weren't poor had wooden beds. Some were big enough for both parents and a few small children, too. They were high, and you would use a footstool to get up into them. Sometimes a cloth was hung above the bed to keep

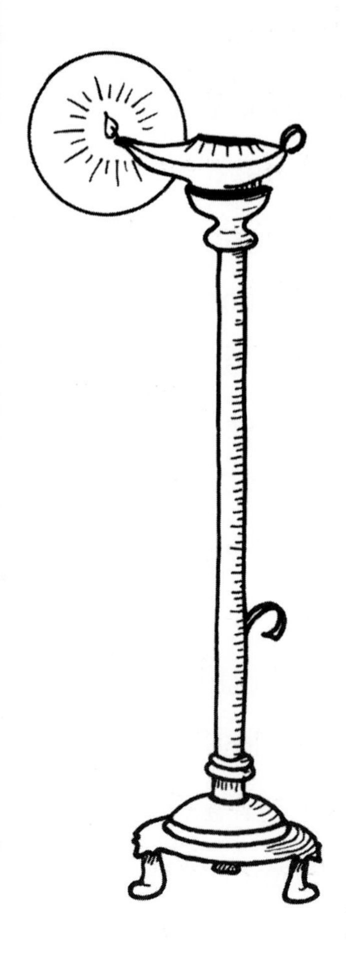

the insects out. There might also be chairs in the house. One kind had three wooden legs and a leather seat. It could be folded up.

At meal time, mats were used instead of chairs. If your family had a wooden table, it would be very low; or your table might be only an animal skin spread out on the ground.

There were some things that every home needed. Every house had lamps. They were usually made of pottery, but they could be metal. Olive oil was poured inside the lamp, and a cloth wick was placed in the oil with the tip sticking up. Then the tip was lit. Most people had a stand to put the lamp on so that it would be high enough.

One lamp was kept burning all night.

The lamps did not burn very brightly. Some lamps had places for several wicks. Even with one of these lamps burning, your house would still be somewhat dark. At night it would be hard to read or sew.

Every home had many pottery or metal containers. Your family would need these things: large jars to store water, large pitchers to carry water from the well, small pitchers and storage jars for wine and oil, storage jars for grain, cooking pots and pans, a bowl and pitcher for washing hands, a large bowl for washing feet, drinking cups, serving bowls, and a very small bowl to hold salt.

Many homes also had bags made of the whole skin of a goat to keep liquids in. Large and small baskets were needed to store and carry things. Of course, every home had a broom.

One of the most important things in the home was the grinding mill. It was made of two large, flat, round stones, one put on top of the other. The grains of wheat or barley were put in a hole on the top. It took two people to move the top stone around. They sat across from each other, and both held onto the wooden handle with one hand. As the stone was turned, flour came out from between the stones. The flour was used to make bread. [3]

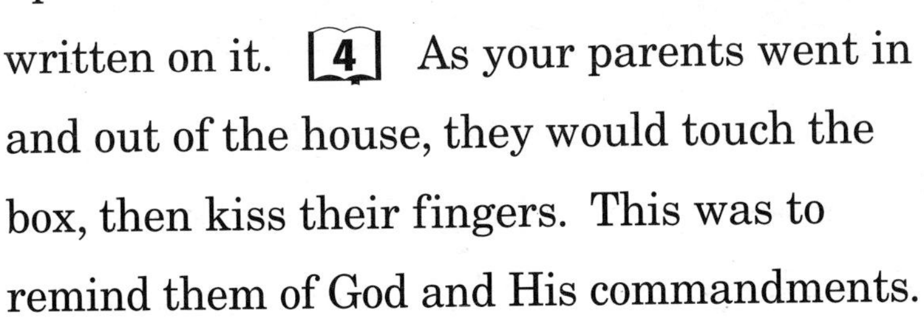

A small metal box called a *Mezuzah* [mĕ-zoo′zŭ] could be found on the door post of many homes. Inside was a folded square of parchment. (Parchment is smooth animal skin, almost like paper.) Special Bible verses were written on it. [4] As your parents went in and out of the house, they would touch the box, then kiss their fingers. This was to remind them of God and His commandments.

There were some families in Palestine that never lived in a house at all. They lived in tents. The tents were made of black goat's hair. The goat-hair cloth kept the family cool in the summer and dry in the winter. Curtains were used to make rooms inside the tent.

Since the tent was moved to different places, only those things that were really needed could be taken along. There are still people today who live in the same kind of goat-hair tent.

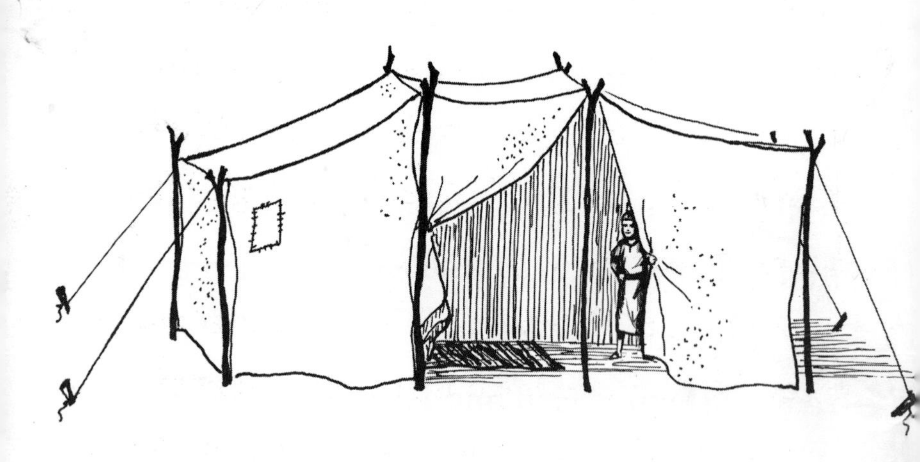

Chapter **2**

What Would the Weather Be Like?

Israel was a land of sunshine and outdoor living. Usually, not one drop of rain would fall from May to September—five whole months! The only moisture during that time was from the dew that came during the night. If you accidentally left something outside overnight, it would be wet with dew in the morning. [5] The dew was good for growing grapes, olives, and figs.

Finally, in October and November some rain would fall and would soften the hard, dry earth. The heaviest rains came in

December, January, and February. It might even snow a little in some high places. March and April brought sunshine and wildflowers. Blooms of all colors covered the hillsides, but the flowers quickly withered when the dry season began again in May.

Refreshing winds often came from the sea in the west, but sometimes hot winds came from the desert in the east and made life miserable. Outside, it was unbearably hot, and sandy dust would blow in your eyes. Inside, it was almost as hot, and even though the shutters on the windows were closed, sand still would get in your food and clothes. There was no place to get away from it. This hot wind still blows in Israel today and is called *Sirocco*.

Chapter 3

What Would Your Family Be Like?

Your mother and father would have been married at a young age. A girl usually got married at thirteen and a boy at about eighteen.

The boy's parents decided which girl he should marry; then they made an agreement with the girl's parents. (If she was really against marrying a certain person, she could say no.)

After a waiting time of about a year, the wedding would take place. The celebrations lasted a whole week, and afterwards the bride and groom went to live with the man's family, or close by them.

When children were born, the parents would think of them all as gifts from God. They would be happier, though, if they had a boy baby. This was because in those days, having a big family was important. Daughters got married and moved away, making the family smaller. But sons brought home their wives and then grandchildren were born into the family, making it even bigger. So, families celebrated more when a son was born.

The newborn baby was washed, rubbed with salt, and then wrapped tightly in *swaddling clothes*. The swaddling was strips of cloth five or six yards long. The wrapped baby could not move his arms or legs. 6

When a baby boy was eight days old, he was named at a special ceremony. The first birthday was remembered, but the family usually did not celebrate any more birthdays after the first one.

When the child was about two, there was another party. This was to celebrate the weaning of the child. This meant that the boy or girl no longer had to be nursed by the mother, but could drink from a cup. [7]

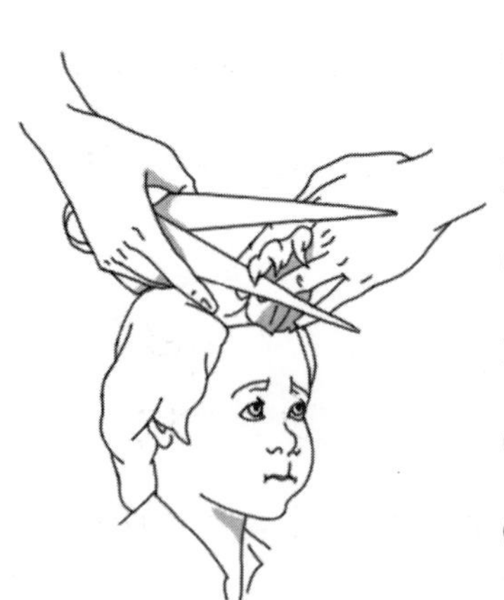

A special celebration was planned when a boy was about four years old. It was the day he would get his first haircut. Friends of the parents came over and helped cut the hair.

Girls did not get haircuts. They always let their hair grow long.

Children were taught always to obey their parents. If you were a child of Israel, you would give special respect to your father, who was the ruler over the family. He ruled over your mother, you and your brothers and sisters, and the servants. And when you had children of your own, he even ruled over them! Since your grandparents probably would live in the same house with you, you would have to obey them as well as your parents.

If you were a boy, your father would teach you some kind of work to do. This was so you could have an honest job when you grew up. When you were twelve, or even before, he would probably teach you to do the same kind of work he did.

You might be a farmer, like many men in Israel, and grow grain, olives, grapes, and figs. Or you might learn to be a carpenter (Jesus' earthly father was one), a weaver, a potter, a bricklayer, a fisher-

man, a tentmaker, a merchant, a metal-smith, a stonecutter, a shepherd, a dyer of cloth, or a tanner (preparer of leather). You might even be a teacher, a doctor, a musician, or a banker.

A father had another important thing to teach his children. He was to teach them about God. About two thousand years before Jesus was born, there lived a great man named Abraham, who trusted in God. God showed Himself to Abraham in a special way and promised to bless all his family. [8] The family grew and grew, and the people who came from Abraham's family were called "Jews." God gave the Jewish people commandments to follow and taught them His laws when He sent Moses to be their leader. [9] These very laws were the things that a Jewish father was to teach his children carefully.

A father also taught his children about an important promise that was given by God. The promise was that some day God would send a Savior who would be born into the family of Abraham. He would be holy and perfect and would take the punishment for the sins of God's people. This Savior would bless not only the Jews, but all the nations of the world. All Jews waited for this promise to come true.

Your mother would take care of you most of the time when you were small. When you were old enough to talk, she might teach you a Bible verse that was

picked out especially for you. She would teach you songs from the book of Psalms in the Bible, other Bible verses, and wise sayings. You would practice them until you could say them without one little mistake!

If your mother knew how, she would teach you to read and write. The language that most people spoke in Israel was called *Aramaic* [ār-ŭ-mā′ĭk].

Unless there were servants in your house, your mother had very little time to play with you. There was so much work for her to do! She had to grind the flour, bake the bread, and do other cooking. She had to spin and weave the wool to make cloth. Then she had to sew the clothes. She also had to mend and wash the clothes, bring the water from the well, find fuel for the fire, and work in the family's vegetable garden. Sometimes she helped her husband with his work, and of course, she took care of the children, too. As girls grew up, they learned from their mothers how to do these jobs.

Chapter **4**

What Would You Wear?

You would probably not have many clothes to choose from when you got dressed. Poor people had only one set of clothes to wear. Only if you were very rich would you have many things to wear. If you wanted to give a generous gift, you might give clothes. They were valuable because it took so much work to make them. [10]

You had to be careful not to get your clothes wet or dirty or torn, because you might not have anything else to change into. When you got a hole in your robe, your mother would patch it, not throw it away. When you got too big for your clothes, they were given to your younger brother or sister. [11]

Clothes could be made with animal skins or with woven cloth. The cloth was made of goat or camel hair, sheep's wool, or flax. Cloth made of goat and camel hair together was called *sackcloth*. It was rough and scratchy.

flax

Flax is a plant with blue flowers that has long, stringy fibers in the stem. These fibers can be woven into a good cloth called *linen*. Fine linen bleached white was one of the most expensive fabrics. A less expensive linen was made of unbleached flax. Linen was also used for candle wicks.

Most clothes were made from either linen or wool, but Jewish law said that the two were not supposed to be mixed together in the same cloth.

If you were a girl, your mother would teach you the important job of spinning and weaving wool. After the wool was taken from the sheep, it had to be washed with soap. Then it was combed, rolled into a rope-like shape, and attached to a spindle. The spindle was a specially shaped stick that helped to twist the rope into strong, even thread. The thread was then put on the loom, where it was woven into cloth.

spindle

Cloth could be made fancy by weaving with different colors of thread on the loom. Stripes or even a checkered design could be woven in. Many women decorated their robes in another way, also. They embroidered designs with a needle and colored thread.

The dyes for coloring the thread came

from interesting places. Purple dye (the most expensive) was made from a gland inside a particular sea snail. Red dye could be made from a certain insect. Yellow was made from the yellow crocus flower, and blue came from the indigo plant.

After the cloth was woven, it had to be sewn into clothes. Most mothers made the clothing for their whole family, sewing with a big needle made of brass or bone.

inner tunic

Three different kinds of robes were worn in Jesus' time. The first kind was the inner tunic. It was like a very long shirt without a collar or buttons. It was usually sleeveless and came to just below the knee. Some rich people wore long ones down to their ankles. They also had long sleeves. Many inner tunics had stripes going down from each shoulder, front and back. This tunic was probably the only thing young children wore most of the time. Also, men who worked hard outside would probably wear only a tunic.

At bedtime you would not have to change clothes, because you would wear your same inner tunic to sleep in. You wouldn't have any pajamas.

Most adults wore another layer of clothes over the inner tunic, especially if they were going somewhere outside the house. They could wear another robe called the *coat tunic.* This

coat tunic

mantle or cloak

tunic was a little longer than the inner tunic. It opened in front like a coat.

The mantle, or cloak, was the heaviest kind of robe. It was especially important to travelers and shepherds, because it kept them warm during the day and was used for a blanket at night. Many people wore a cloak over their inner tunic for their everyday dress. Your mother would make sure you had a warm cloak to wear in the rainy months.

Girls and women wore the same kinds of robes as men, only theirs were a little longer and fancier. Sometimes a woman's mantle would have a design like this woven into it at the corners.

A man's mantle might have a special stripe around the bottom of it that looked like this:

This was one way to tell the difference between a woman's clothes and a man's. A man would be ashamed to wear a woman's robe.

A man's mantle was supposed to have fringes at each of the four corners, with one blue thread in each fringe. The blue thread was to remind him of the Law of God.

If you were sick, your mother might tie little bundles of seeds, herbs, or spices into your robe. This was supposed to make you better.

An important piece of clothing that was worn with the inner tunic or coat tunic was the girdle. It was like a wide belt. Usually it was made of linen and wrapped several times around the waist. In the folds of your girdle you could keep money, snacks, and other small things. You could also tuck the bottom of your tunic into the girdle if you needed to run or work. This was called "girding your loins."

When a person wore a girdle, a pouch was made in the top part of the tunic where the front edges overlapped. You could carry larger things there. Sometimes a shepherd would tuck a baby lamb in this place.

It was important to keep the sun off your head in very hot weather. Men usually wore a hat called a turban, made of cloth wound around the head. Sometimes

a cloth was worn that went over the head and also hung down the neck and back. A man did not feel fully dressed without something on his head.

Women wore veils on their heads whenever they went out. They even wore veils in their own house when they had company. Sometimes it was hard to tell who was under

the veils if the face was covered. You might not even recognize your own mother! Jewish women did not always have their whole face covered by the veil, but they sometimes hid their face when they saw a man coming.

Women and girls took a lot of trouble with their hair, even though it was usually covered. It was always long. Some ladies braided their hair in many braids or wound it around their head in a fancy design. They used combs or even gum to make the hair stay where they wanted it. [12]

Men sometimes cut their hair, but they liked their beard to be long. They only trimmed it a little to keep it neat. They were very proud of their hair and beard. Sometimes they put olive oil on both their hair and beard.

Women also used olive oil. They put it on their face every day to keep the skin soft. Sometimes it was mixed with expensive perfume and sweet-smelling spices. [13]

Some ladies painted their eyes with black make-up, using a polished metal mirror to see themselves. They even might have put makeup on the eyes of their children, thinking it would bring good luck. Ladies also used red makeup to make their cheeks look rosy.

Women and girls enjoyed wearing jewelry. They could wear earrings, necklaces, anklets, combs, bracelets, and even nose rings. The jewelry could be made of gold, silver, pearls, ivory, precious stones, or glass. Coins were sometimes used for jewelry, too.

The signet ring was one kind of jewelry that men wore. A man had his own design on his ring. When he pressed his ring in wax or clay, the design would make its mark, and it would be like he had signed his name.

Almost everyone wore sandals on his

feet. They usually were made of leather or wood on the bottom and were strapped to the feet with strips of leather called *latchets.* You would take off your shoes every time you went inside. The custom was to take off or put on your right sandal first.

If you went barefoot, you had to be careful not to step on a scorpion or centipede. They both have painful stings.

scorpion

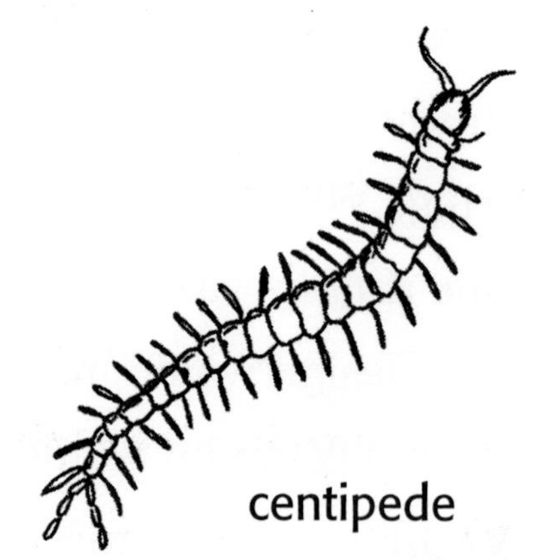

centipede

Chapter **5**

What Would You Eat?

pomegranate

Most of your food would be grown in your own garden or in the village fields. You would eat lettuce, cucumbers, dandelions, melons, pomegranates, beans, lentils, peas, and onions from your garden. Oranges, dates, walnuts, almonds, and pistachio nuts grew on trees in the land of Israel. Figs and grapes were the favorite fruits. They could be eaten fresh in the summer and fall, or they could be dried on the rooftops for winter eating. Sometimes raisins and figs were pressed together into "cakes." The dried figs could also be strung on a rope and hung in your house until they were needed.

Most of the grapes were squeezed for their juice. The juice had to be strained before it was served to be sure there were no bits of grape or insects in it. Grape juice could also be used to make grape-honey. The juice was boiled until it was thick and sweet like honey. You could eat it on bread like jam.

Bread spread with bee's honey and butter mixed together was a treat that children especially liked.

Olive oil was an important food. You would eat it on your bread and vegetables the way we use butter. Your mother would also use lots of it in the things she cooked. [14] The food she cooked would not be plain. The women were very good at making different flavored sauces and using tasty spices.

Meat was not eaten very often. If you lived near a place to fish, you could have fresh fish. Other people ate fish that had been dried and salted so that it would not spoil. Eggs were often eaten. For a special meal, you might have goat's meat. A lamb or a calf would only be cooked for the most important celebrations. [15]

Your milk might come from a goat, a sheep, a cow, or a camel! You could drink it fresh, or it could be used to make butter, cheese, or a food that looked like lumpy yogurt.

Bread was the most important food in Israel. It was eaten at every meal. Bread was never cut with a knife but had to be broken into pieces with the hands. When you said that you "broke bread," you meant that you ate a meal. Bread could be made of barley or wheat flour. It could be baked into big, round loaves that looked like stones, or into small biscuits or paper-thin pancakes. It could be made into fancy cakes with seeds, nuts, honey, or grape-honey. Bread made without yeast, or leaven, was called *unleavened bread.* It was flat and heavy.

The bread could be baked in the big town oven or at home. Your mother might have an oven that looked like a big pottery jar. There was a hole at the bottom to build a fire. She put the bread in through the hole at the top, and the loaves cooked on shelves inside the oven.

For cooking the rest of the meal, your mother could put her pots right over a fire, or she might have a clay stove. The clay stove would have a hole near the bottom where the fire was built and holes on the top to rest the pots.

Your mother would have stone measuring cups, frying pans, large stew pots, and

casserole dishes with lids that fit perfectly. All her pots would be black on the bottom from the fire and smoke. Some homes had a special jar for boiling water. Hot coals were put into a hole at the bottom, and the water was heated in the top part of the jar.

Breakfast and lunch were more like snacks than meals. You would have bread, of course, and perhaps some fruit or olives and cheese or dried fish.

Your mother would get out her pots and pans in the afternoon so she could cook a hot meal to serve after sunset. She might make vegetable stew, lentils, or cooked fish for dinner.

Before eating, everyone had to wash his hands in a special way. You would hold your hands over a wide bowl while someone else poured water over them. There might be a place on the bowl to keep a piece of olive-oil soap and a special place in the bottom where the dirty water drained.

A towel for drying was put on your shoulder.

Also before eating, your family would give thanks to God. This is probably what the prayer would be like: "Blessed art thou, Jehovah our God, King of the world, who causes bread to come forth from the earth." Everyone would say "Amen" at the end. 16

The men and boys ate first. The women and girls served them and then ate what was left.

You would sit on the floor during the meal. At your place would be some bread and perhaps a colored glass. (Only rich people bought expensive clear glass.) There would be no knife, fork, spoon, or plate. How could you eat the food? If it wasn't too juicy, you could pick up pieces with your fingers. The bread was used to scoop up gravies and sauces. Everyone ate the food right from the serving bowl.

If you were a guest at someone's house, the father might take a piece of broken bread that had been dipped into the food, or a piece of meat, and put it into your mouth. This bite of food was called a sop. It was given to show friendship. [17]

After eating, the family said another prayer of thanks. Then you would wash your hands again the same way as before the meal, because they would be dirty! All the cooked food was usually eaten, but if there were leftovers, they would be thrown to the dogs. There were no refrigerators to keep the food from spoiling.

Chapter 6

What Kinds of Chores Would You Have?

There were some chores that had to be done every day. Every day children helped find things to burn in the fire. It was hard to find enough sticks. Sometimes dried grass, flowers, or thorns had to be used.

If you were a girl, you would learn how to get water from the well. Every evening you would take a big pottery pitcher, a leather bucket, and a rope with you to the well. You would let the bucket down into the water on the rope, and you would pour the water you drew up into the pitcher. [18]

Then the full pitcher had to be balanced on

your head, shoulder, or hip. Girls sometimes used a pad if they were going to carry the pitcher on their head. The pitcher was heavy and easy to break. Sometimes girls came home without the water, because their pitcher had broken.

Your mother might ask you to get some embers to start the fire for cooking dinner. You would take a piece of broken pottery and go to the village baker. The old ashes were raked out of his oven in the evening. He would give you some burnt pieces of wood that were still glowing, and you would carry them home carefully in your piece of pottery.

Sifting the grain was another chore that children could help with. You would put the grain into a sieve, which looked like a basket with holes in the bottom. As you shook the sieve, the good grain fell down through the holes. The straw (chaff) would stay on top as well as pebbles and poisonous seeds. The good grain was washed and spread out to dry on a sheet on the rooftop. The dried grain was kept in large pottery containers.

If you were a boy, you might have the job of a shepherd and watch the family sheep. You would take the sheep to safe places to eat and drink, and you would protect them from thieves and wild animals. Sometimes girls got the job of watching a flock of goats.

If your mother was making butter, she would probably ask you to help. She would pour milk into a goatskin bag. Then she would hang it from some poles stuck in the ground. Your job would be to jiggle, shake, and poke the bag until the milk turned into butter.

Grape picking was more like a party than work. When the grapes were ready to pick in September, families moved into tents or leafy huts in the vineyards. Men, women, and children gathered the grapes into baskets. The workers liked to sing while they picked.

After picking the grapes, the children could also help make them into juice. The grapes were put into what looked like a small wading pool carved out of rock.

Below was a smaller pool, where the juice drained. Everyone walked around in the pool, smashing the grapes with their feet. You would sing and clap to the music while you smashed, being careful not to fall. Your feet and legs would be purple for a long time afterward, but it would be fun.

Another fun job was picking olives. In November, your whole family would go with baskets to collect the ripe olives from your trees. The olives that had fallen to the ground were picked up first; then the branches were shaken or beaten with a stick until the rest of the olives fell down. Most of the olives were pressed with heavy weights to make oil.

Chapter 7

What Would School Be Like?

Boys began school when they were about six. Girls did not go to school, because people felt that girls did not need to know the kinds of things that were taught in school. School was held in the neighborhood synagogue [sĭn′ŭ-gŏg], which was like a church.

There were about twenty-five boys in each class. The teacher sat on a stool, the older students on a low bench, and the younger ones sat on mats on the floor.

The Old Testament, part of the Bible, was the only book that the boys used until they were ten years old. The Old Testament was written on rolled-up scrolls in the

Hebrew language. Since the children spoke Aramaic at home, they had to learn Hebrew before they could read the Bible. After studying the Bible, the older boys would learn the Jewish laws that were not in the Bible.

At the age of twelve or thirteen, most boys finished school.

The main way of learning was to memorize things by repeating out loud after the teacher. People walking by the synagogue could hear the boys' voices, and the parents would know that their children were learning.

The teachers used little wooden boards covered with wax to write on. They drew letters on the wax with a pointed stick, and when the board was full, they smoothed the wax and wrote on it again.

A boy might have his own little scroll with a few verses written on it. He could take this home to study.

Boys went to school every day of the week, but on Saturday, the day of rest, they only reviewed their lessons and had no new ones. They went to school two times every day, once early in the morning, and then later in the afternoon. Between ten in the morning and three in the afternoon there was no school, because that was the hottest part of the day.

Here are some rules a teacher was supposed to follow:

- A teacher was to keep all the promises he made.
- If a student did not understand, a teacher was not to get impatient, but was to explain more clearly.
- If a student needed to be punished, he could be spanked with a strap, but not with a stick.
- During the hottest months of the summer, there could be only four hours of school. Also during this time teachers were not allowed to punish the students.

Chapter 8

What Would You Do for Fun?

Children were expected to do their share of work around the home, but there was always some time for play. Here are some things you might have done for fun:

- You could gather wild-flowers on the hills in the spring.
- If you had a hook and string, you could go fishing.
- You could go swimming. (Most parents

taught their children to swim.)

- You might go to the market-place to look around or meet friends.

- You and your friends could play games with a leather ball stuffed with bran.
- You could play with a pet bird.
- If you lived near a main road, it would be fun to watch groups of travelers on their camels and donkeys. (A group of people traveling together like that was called a *caravan*. A large caravan could be 200 camels long. Jesus lived near one of these caravan roads.)

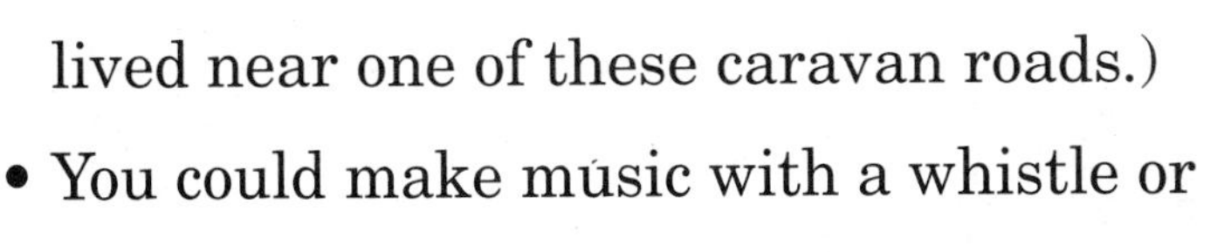

- You could make music with a whistle or a flute.
- You could practice hitting a target with your sling shot. 19

- You and your friends might make up and guess riddles.
- You could look for buried treasure. (People in the Holy Land sometimes buried their money to keep it safe. Once in a while, the owner would not return to uncover it.)
- You might pretend to be grown up and have a wedding or a funeral.
- You could play with toys. Very young children had clay rattles of different shapes, perhaps a doll or a bird. Some girls had doll houses, complete with small clay pots and pans, clay furniture, and clay dolls. Some of the dolls could even move their arms and legs.

Chapter 9

How Would You Worship God?

When a boy turned thirteen, he was then thought to be a man. Before his birthday, he had to learn by heart twenty special verses from the Old Testament. [20] These verses were called the *Shema* (shmaw—rhymes with *law*). All men were supposed to say the Shema in the morning before they did any work or ate any food. They also said it every evening. Before doing this, a man had to wash his hands and face. Then he put his mantle over his head. (The mantle had to have the special fringe on it.) He also strapped boxes called *phylacteries* [fĭ-lăk′ter-ēz] onto his forehead and left arm. Inside these leather boxes were

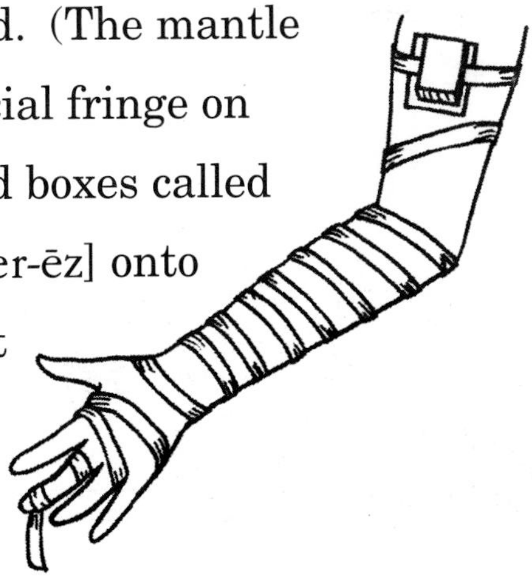

Scripture verses to remind the man to keep God's laws.

There were some men who wore their phylacteries all the time. Their phylacteries were very big, and the fringes on their mantles were very long. These men were called *Pharisees*. They felt they were very holy, and they liked to make up laws for everyone to follow. Jesus said that they were not really holy, but were proud showoffs.

One of God's commandments was that the seventh day should be a day of rest. The Jews counted Saturday as the seventh day and called it the *Sabbath* (meaning "rest"). The Sabbath began on Friday evening after sunset and lasted until the sun went down on Saturday.

On this day, no one could work.

The Pharisees made lots of rules about what was work and what was not. One rule said that you could only walk a certain short distance on the Sabbath. Another rule said that a lady could not look in the mirror on the Sabbath because she might see a gray hair and pull it out. That would be work.

Friday was called the *Day of Preparation*. Around three o'clock in the afternoon, the women began to prepare the food for the Sabbath, because no cooking could be done after the sun went down. The men did all the chores that needed to be done, so that they could rest the next day. Everyone washed up and dressed in their best clothes. A special Sabbath lamp was lit when the sun went down, and the family ate their Sabbath dinner. The food might be cold, but it was the best meal of the week.

Early Saturday morning, the whole family went to the synagogue. The men would be sure to wash their hands and feet before they entered the building. There were places with water near the synagogue where a man could do this, and there might even be a place nearby to take a bath.

As you walked into the synagogue, you would see on both sides of the room sets of long stone benches that went up like wide stairways. If you sat on the top bench, you could see everything in the synagogue. At the far end was a carved chest called an *ark,* which held the rolled-up scrolls of the Old Testament Scriptures. A lamp which was always lit hung above it. There were many lamps and candlesticks in the room. A candlestick with seven branches always could be found in a Jewish synagogue. In the middle of the synagogue was a raised platform. On top

of that was a pulpit. The reader of the Scriptures would lay the scrolls there while he read.

Every week in the synagogue, two different parts from the Old Testament were read. Several men took turns reading. Then a man who had been chosen that week would explain to the people the meaning of the Scriptures. He sat down while he spoke. There would also be many prayers and blessings. The service ended just before lunch time. 21

Your family would celebrate many holidays and feast days every year. There was a celebration every month, when a new moon appeared in the night sky. Bonfires were lit on the hilltops to let everyone know when the moon was first seen.

The three most important feasts were the Feast of Tabernacles, Passover, and the Feast of Pentecost. If you lived close to Jerusalem, your whole family might go there for all three feasts, because the Temple of the Jews was there.

Tabernacle means "dwelling place." The Feast of Tabernacles was celebrated to

remind the Jewish people that their ancestors lived in tents in the desert. It was a happy time for all. Your family would build a booth outside, perhaps in the garden. The booth would be made of a stick frame covered with leafy branches. Everyone in the family would camp out there for a week.

The Feast of Tabernacles was celebrated in the fall, after all the figs, grapes, and olives had been harvested. Thanks was given to God, and prayers were made for enough rain to fall in the coming year. During the feast week, those who came to the Temple to worship (including children) carried branches of palm and other trees, and waved them during the singing of the Psalms.

Passover was another time for remembering the past. The first Passover was in Egypt, where God's people were slaves. God had promised to free them and bring them to a land of their own (Israel), but the Pharaoh (king) of Egypt would not let them go.

This is what God did: He told Moses to tell his people to put the blood of a perfect male lamb on the doorposts of their house, then to roast the lamb and eat it with unleavened bread and bitter herbs. Later that night, the angel of death passed over all the homes in Egypt. He did no harm at the houses with blood on the doorposts, but at the houses without the blood, the first-born child died. Then Pharaoh let God's people go. 22

The Passover feast was held every year

in April. Everyone who could went to Jerusalem for the week of Passover.

Pentecost (also called the "Feast of Weeks") was always held fifty days after Passover. The Pentecost celebration was held during the time when all the barley and wheat had been harvested. No one worked on the day of celebration. Two special loaves of new wheat bread were given to God at the Temple. The men brought offerings of the best grain from their crops to thank the Lord for His goodness. [23]

Chapter **10**

A Passover Visit to Jerusalem

The trip to Jerusalem for Passover was an exciting adventure for Jewish children. Here is a story of one boy's first visit to Jerusalem: 24

Joshua was hot, tired, and dusty as he walked up the Mount of Olives, the last hill on the road to Jerusalem. He had been walking uphill all day. Five days ago he had left Nazareth in a large caravan which included his parents and his Uncle Reuben and Aunt Rebekah. His younger sister, Esther, had stayed home with Grandmother.

The roads were dusty, uneven, and full of rocks. Since he was nine years old, Joshua was too big to ride in a box strapped to the side of a donkey like some of the smaller children. It was fun, though, to walk along with so many friends and relatives. Sometimes everyone sang Psalms together as they hiked.

When Joshua came to the top of the hill, he got his first look at the great city of Jerusalem. The tops of hundreds of buildings could be seen behind the walls of the city.

As they walked down the hill, he saw beautiful homes and well-kept gardens. He also saw people setting up tents.

"I'm glad we don't have to spend Passover in a tent, Father," said Joshua.

"Yes, it was very kind of our friends in Jerusalem to invite us to stay in their home," answered his father. "The townspeople are very generous in that way, but there is not enough room in the city for all the visitors."

When the caravan got near the city wall, Joshua saw that some of the stones in

it were gigantic. "This strong wall was built to protect the city," Uncle Reuben explained. "You can get inside only through one of the gates. They are made of thick wood covered with metal, so they will be strong enough to keep enemies out. Did you notice that each gate has a tower for the watchman?"

"Let us hurry," urged Aunt Rebekah. "The gates will be closed at sunset."

"Even if the gates were closed, we could still get inside, Joshua," explained his father. "Each gate has a small door cut into it, just big enough for a man to crawl through. The gatekeeper would open it for you. But since the donkeys cannot get in that way, we had better hurry."

After walking through the gate, Joshua noticed that he was standing in a stone hallway. It was shady and cool there, and there were benches to sit on. A few steps beyond was the city he had heard so many stories about.

The streets, which were neatly paved with large, flat stones, led Joshua and his family by the most magnificent buildings he had ever seen.

The huge fortress of Antonia, where the Roman soldiers stayed, looked to Joshua like a whole town itself. He could imagine being in one of the four giant towers and looking down upon the whole city of Jerusalem.

Then they passed the grand palace of Herod (who had been a ruler in Israel). "I've heard," remarked Joshua's mother, "that the guest rooms in the palace are so large that one hundred people can sleep in each one! Wouldn't it be fun to see all the covered porches, the walkways, the canals filled with water, and the courtyards full of trees and flowers? And, oh yes, those statues that actually spout water! Can you imagine?"

As he walked through the city, Joshua saw many other wonderful palaces, high towers, large meeting places, and synagogues decorated with carved stone. But for him, the most amazing sight in all Jerusalem was the beautiful Temple of the Jews. It rose high above the city on a huge stone platform. The top part of the Temple shone so brightly that it almost made Joshua's eyes hurt. He couldn't wait to visit there.

It seemed to Joshua that the city was alive with people. He saw rich women wearing robes with gold threads woven in them and mantles trimmed with fur. He saw Roman soldiers with their swords, sick and crippled people begging for money, Pharisees praying on the street corners,

slaves being brought in to be sold at the market-place, strangers from far countries, and visitors from all over Israel who had come, like himself, into Jerusalem for the Passover.

Passing through the streets were horse-drawn chariots carrying people, carts packed with things to sell pulled by donkeys, and men carrying huge bundles on their backs. Everyone seemed to be going to the marketplace just ahead. When they got there, Joshua was amazed. "I've never seen things like this in the market at Nazareth!" he exclaimed. "You could buy anything you needed here!"

"Yes, and even things you didn't need!" laughed his mother.

There was glass from Sidon; fine fabrics from Babylonia and India; spices, precious stones, and gold from Arabia; beautiful and expensive jewelry; and rare perfumes and ointments. The sellers made a great deal of noise as they shouted to all who passed, "My goods are the finest you can buy!"

Joshua's family found their friend's house in a quiet part of the city, away from the busy marketplace. The gate at the street was very plain. His father knocked at the door. A servant came to the gate and asked, "Who?" Joshua's father answered only, "I." Since his voice was recognized as a friend's, the servant let everyone into the passageway and led them to the front room. Joshua remembered to take off his sandals before he went in.

The inside of the house looked like no home Joshua had ever seen in Nazareth. On the floor was a design made of hundreds of tiny different-colored tiles. On the ceiling were wood panels carved with more designs. There were also lines and squares painted on the walls. There were some large chairs with backs, couches you could lie down on, and heavy curtains at the sides of the window. Through the window he could see the courtyard. It was paved with marble and planted with palm, pomegranate, and evergreen trees.

The owners of the house came into the room. They were glad to see Joshua's family. "Peace to you, Simeon, and to your family," the man said. Then he kissed Joshua's father on both cheeks.

"And peace to you," replied his father. The man spoke to the servant in a low voice, and the servant left. His wife brought glasses of cool water for everyone. The glasses were made of perfectly clear glass, and Joshua's mother remarked how lovely they were. Joshua was very careful with his.

The servant came back carrying a large copper bowl, a pitcher of water, and some

towels on his shoulder. One by one, he washed and dried each person's feet. The cool water felt good on Joshua's hot feet. 25

That night, preparations for the Passover started. The father of the home lit a candle, and without saying one word looked throughout the house for leaven (the yeast used in making bread). It all had to be thrown out, and only unleavened bread could be eaten at Passover and a whole week afterward.

The blowing of the Temple trumpets woke Joshua the next morning. There were many things to do, because Passover was that night. The women had to see that the food was bought and prepared. Joshua's mother made sure the family's clothing was clean and mended for the feast. She had made Joshua a new robe that he would wear for the first time at Passover. Everyone took a bath that day. There was actually a special room in the house that had a built-in bathtub!

The men had an important job to do.

They needed to go to the Temple to sacrifice the Passover lamb, which had been kept outside in a pen. It was a perfectly white male lamb, less than a year old. Joshua's father said he could help take the lamb to the Temple.

The Temple was bigger and more beautiful than Joshua had ever imagined. 26 As they climbed the stairs leading up to the Temple, he could look down and see the streets of the lower city. He noticed that most of the people going up with them were wearing clean, white robes. Before entering, everyone took off their sandals. Inside, Joshua saw the huge Court of the Gentiles. (*Gentile* means one who is not a Jew. Everyone could go into the Court of the Gentiles.) The ground was paved with marble of different colors. At the sides were porches with tall white marble columns. In there, Joshua watched

men selling animals for sacrifice and men changing the money of different countries into the money of the Temple. [27]

Only Jews could go into the middle part of the Temple. After Joshua and his father and uncle climbed the stairs to this part, they passed through a giant brass gate. "This is called the *Beautiful Gate*," explained Uncle Reuben. "It's so heavy that

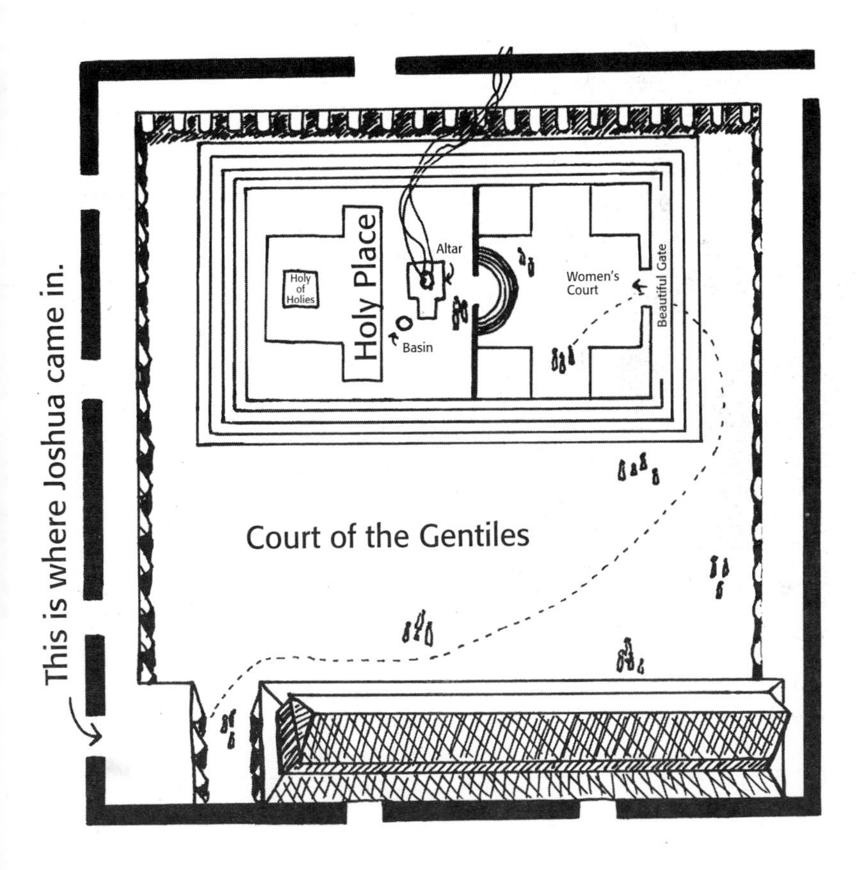

it takes twenty men to open it!" 28

the Holy Place

Once through the gate, they were in the Women's Court. It was called that because women could go no further into the Temple. Joshua stayed there and waited while the men took the lamb up some curved steps and further inside. While he was waiting, he listened to a group of men and children sing Psalms on the steps. Some other men were playing musical instruments.

Joshua could see the smoke from the fat of the lambs being burned on the altar inside. He knew that the blood had been sprinkled on the altar and that the meat was to be taken home and cooked for the Passover feast.

When his father and uncle returned, they told Joshua what they had seen inside: a big stone altar, a huge brass bowl on the backs of twelve lions (used by the priests for washing), and the Holy Place made of giant white marble stones covered by gold. "Do you remember my telling you about the Holy of Holies, Joshua?" asked his father. "It's inside the Holy Place, behind a thick curtain. 29 Only the High Priest can go in there once a year."

That evening, Joshua's family and friends gathered in the banquet room of the house, wearing their finest clothes. They gave thanks to God, and the feast began, the men lying down on special banquet couches. The feast was like a ceremony. Each food was eaten at a special time, with prayers, hymns, and washing of hands in between. This is what

the women served: the lamb, which had been roasted whole; unleavened bread; bitter herbs; and a sauce made with vinegar, raisins, and dates.

It was late when everyone was finished eating. Some incense was put on the hot coals of a burner, and Joshua suddenly felt sleepy as the spicy smell of cinnamon filled the room. He was tired, but happy to be included for the first time in the Passover feast at Jerusalem.

The last Passover feast that Jesus ate with His disciples was a very special one. We call it the *Last Supper.* It took place the night before Jesus died on the cross. When the unleavened bread and the fruit of the vine were served, Jesus said they were like His body and blood. He knew that He would be hung on the cross the next day. Jesus also knew that He would come back to life after three days and that He could give eternal life also to all those who believed in Him. By dying, Jesus took the punishment for the sins of those who believed, so that they, too, could live forever with God.

When we have the Lord's Supper (or communion) at church, we think of the death of Jesus and what it means for us. This is what we do instead of Passover, because Jesus is our perfect Passover Lamb.

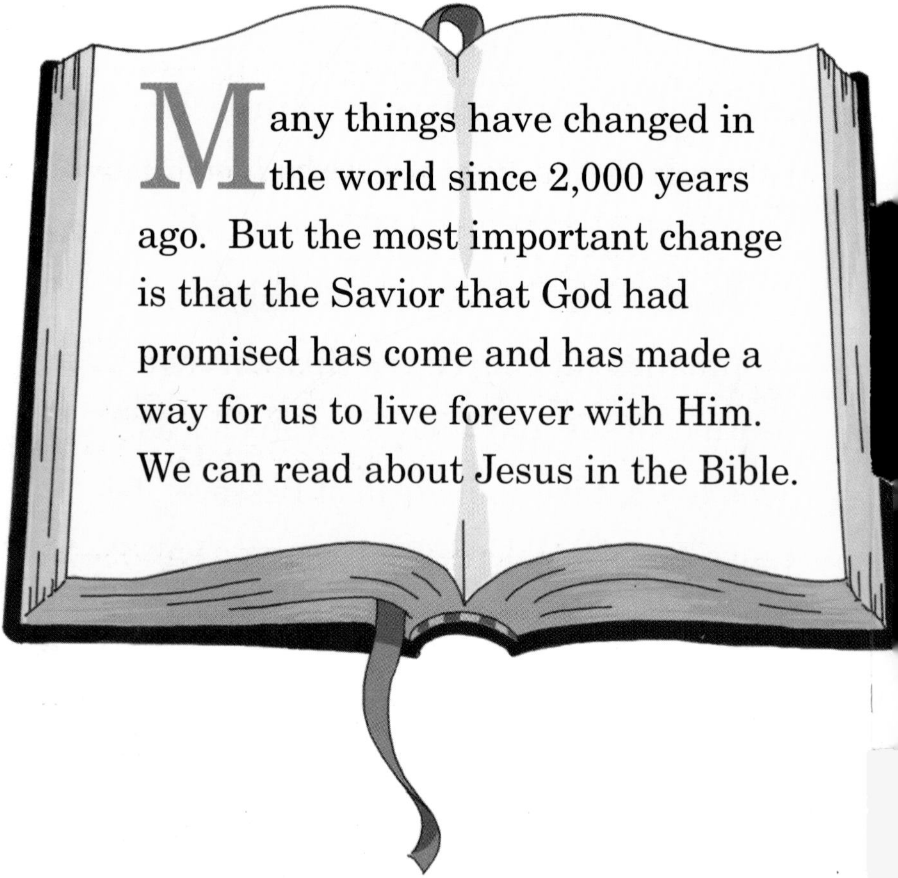

Many things have changed in the world since 2,000 years ago. But the most important change is that the Savior that God had promised has come and has made a way for us to live forever with Him. We can read about Jesus in the Bible.

DIRECTORY OF BIBLE STORIES

1 Maybe this is the kind of floor in which the coin got lost in Luke 15:8–10. See two things the woman did to find the coin.

2 Jesus told a story about what might happen after a family had all gotten in bed: Luke 11:5–9.

3 Jesus said that when He comes again there will be two women doing this. See what happens to them in Matthew 24:41.

4 These were the verses: Deuteronomy 6:4–9 and 11:18–21.

5 A man named Gideon asked God a question. God answered it with dew: Judges 6:37–40.

6 This is what Jesus wore after He was born. The story of His birth is in Luke 2:1–16.

7 Abraham had a big feast when Isaac was weaned, but something spoiled the party. See Genesis 21:8–11.

8 Read what God said to Abraham in Genesis 17:1–8.

9 In Exodus 20 you can read about how God gave His commandments to Moses.

10 Samson offered a wonderful prize to whoever could solve his riddle. See Judges 14:12–14.

11 Jesus said we should not worry about having enough clothes to wear. Why? Read Matthew 6:28–30.

12 The Bible tells how to be beautiful without having a fancy hairdo: 1 Peter 3:3–4 (*plaiting* means braiding).

13 Some said Mary wasted the expensive perfume. What do you think? John 12:3–9.

14 Read a story about a pot of oil that never got empty: 2 Kings 4:1–7.

15 A fatted calf was eaten at this happy celebration: Luke 15:12–32.

16 Perhaps this is what Jesus said when He blessed the loaves and fishes in Matthew 14:16–21. Find out what amazing thing happened to the food.

17 At His Last Supper, Jesus gave a sop to someone. You may be surprised at who it was: John 13:26.

18 Once Jesus wanted a drink but had no bucket or rope. Find out whom He asked to help Him in John 4:6–14.

19 Here is the story of a boy who was really a good shot with his sling: 1 Samuel 17:40–50.

20 These are the verses they had to learn: Deuteronomy 6:4–9, Deuteronomy 11:13–21, and Numbers 15:37–41.

21 One time Jesus preached in the synagogue at Nazareth and the people didn't like what He said. Find out what they tried to do in Luke 4:16–30.

22 You can read this story in Exodus 12:1–51.

23 Acts chapter 2 tells the very surprising story of what happened on one Day of Pentecost.

24 Jesus went to Jerusalem when He was twelve. His parents thought He had gotten lost there. Read Luke 2:41–51 to find out where He was found.

25 A servant quite often did this job, but see who did the foot-washing in John 13:3–5.

26 Jesus told His disciples what would happen to that beautiful Temple in Mark 13:1 and 2. A few years later it did come true, just as Jesus said.

27 It made Jesus angry to see men selling things in the Temple, the place for worshiping God. Read Matthew 21:12 to see what He did about it.

28 Peter and John attracted a big crowd when they did a miracle at this gate in Acts 3:1–11.

29 Find out what happened to this curtain (veil) on the day that Jesus died on the cross: Matthew 27:51.